Nicholas' Values

A Child's Guide to Building Character

Sharon Scott, LPC, LMFT
with Nicholas, the Cocker Spaniel

Illustrated by
George Phillips

HRD Press
Amherst, Massachusetts

Published by Human Resource Development Press, Inc.
22 Amherst Road
Amherst, Massachusetts 01002
(413) 253-3488
1-800-822-2801 (U.S. and Canada)
(413) 253-3490 (fax)
http://www.hrdpress.com

ISBN 0-87425-665-8

Dedicated With Love to My Family and Friends From Childhood

When I was growing up, the average child had 10 to 14 significant adults involved in his or her upbringing. I was fortunate to have many more! I would like to thank the following adults who, during my youth, helped to teach me good values:

Harry Jr. and Johnny Scott

Harry Sr. and Audrey Scott

Smith and Maggie Nicholson

Kenneth and Virginia Henderson

Monroe and Verna Harris

Leon and Bernice John

Finis and Hazel McFarland

Robert and Mary Nicholson

John and Selma Robinson

Jenny Nicholson

Frank and Lizzie Nicholson

Johnny Cates

Nat and Ella Edmonson

Fred and Reba Sneed

Janet Wilkinson

Ralph and Frances Williams

Don Rice

Herman and Billie Mindlin

Martha Cope

Jim and Mary Jo Woods

E. C. Coffey

"Smut" and Mary Smith

"Speedy" and Ruby Robison

Rev. Walter Underwood

Henry and Verda Smith

Mildred Fuller

Hazel Scalf

Victor and Martha Marie Whitfield

Marcie Hudel

I would also like to thank the following teachers:

Emalee Sumerlin, Lillian Johnson, Pauline Riley Harris, Suzanne Hall, Glee Robertson, Ireta Cady, Winnie Fae Fitzhugh, Abner Ragsdale, Ruth West, and Fred Caldwell.

Sadly, the average child of today has only one to four significant adults involved in his or her upbringing.

Other Books by Sharon Scott and Nicholas, the Cocker Spaniel

Life's Not Always Fair: A Child's Guide to Managing Emotions

Too Smart for Trouble

Not Better . . . Not Worse . . . Just Different

Too Cool for Drugs (co-authored by Dr. Wayne Hindmarsh)

Other Books by Sharon Scott

How to Say No and Keep Your Friends, 2nd Edition

Peer Pressure Reversal: An Adult Guide to Developing a Responsible Child, 2nd Edition

When to Say Yes! And Make More Friends

Positive Peer Groups

TABLE OF CONTENTS

ABOUT THE AUTHORS

Sharon Scott is a licensed professional counselor and marriage and family therapist whose internationally recognized work has been making a difference in people's lives for over 30 years. She has provided dynamic skills-based workshops and keynotes on many topics to over one million people across the United States and globally in South Africa, Australia, Canada, Spain, Switzerland, Turkey, Malaysia, and Micronesia. Her eight widely acclaimed books have served as guidance for nearly a generation of children and their parents. Prior to opening her company, LifeSkills for Positive Living, in 1980, she was Director of the nationally recognized First Offender Program of the Dallas Police Department. For over four years, she also provided social-work services for the Dallas County Department of Human Services.

In 2001, the Texas Counseling Association honored Sharon with the Molly Gerold Human Rights Award for over 20 years of worldwide volunteer efforts in drug prevention. She has appeared on CNN and *Good Morning, Australia*, and has been quoted in numerous publications and other media, including *The London Times, Redbook, Teen Magazine, 20/20, Good Housekeeping, The Washington Post,* and *The Dallas Morning News*.

Nicholas, Sharon's beloved Cocker Spaniel, has assisted her in all five of the books in her elementary-age series. He has served as a pet-therapy dog, visiting the elderly in nursing homes, and has been a volunteer with the Humane Society, bestowing "nose kisses" in return for donations to help homeless animals! A graduate of dog-obedience class, he earned a Ph.D. (that's "PuppyHood Degree"!) from Richland College. He is listed in the 1995 edition of *Who's Who of Animals*.

Nicholas and Sharon were honored with the 1995 and 1998 TCA Professional Writing Award for their previous books.

PREFACE

Times are changing! And not always for the better when it comes to children. Time, technology, and tension are interfering with our family time. It's been said that, on average, children in grade five or higher spend more waking, communicating hours with peers and media than they do with their parents! By the time kids graduate from high school, they've sat in front of a television 1,200 more hours than they've sat in a classroom. And we wonder why values are changing.

Children watch too many television programs that promote violence, sarcasm, cutthroat competition, materialism, putdowns, and general negativity. They may listen to musicians who dress provocatively and advocate unhealthy lifestyles. They may observe adults using radar detectors so they can break laws and not get caught speeding. They see road rage. They hear about "ethically challenged" politicians who are supposed to be our leaders. They often hear adults gossip about friends and neighbors. They are smitten with "affluenza," which we adults sometimes encourage. Brand labels are so important to them that self-esteem is linked to a wardrobe rather than to personal integrity and achievement.

Children live in a fast-paced world, one that doesn't always encourage them to stop and think about the other people with whom they share this world. Popular maxims such as "Me first," "The best defense is a good offense," and "The person with the most toys when he dies, wins" all exemplify attitudes that do not teach children how to live ethical lives.

Frankly, this situation has left many children confused. They hear about the importance of values, and are told what values they should have, but they don't always see adults respecting those values and demonstrating them.

In an effort to help children develop and maintain a healthy attitude and lifestyle, Nicholas and I have lovingly selected eight basic values that all people would want for children. They emphasize being nice, involved, confident, honest, obedient, loyal, and accountable, and, of course, sharing. I hope this book brings joy to the lives of your children or students as they grow toward adulthood with good, strong characters!

I would also like to extend special thanks to the following people who helped me greatly in the preparation of this book: George Phillips for his delightful illustrations; Mary George for her fabulous job as editor; Elizabeth Luse, Ph.D., professor and literacy specialist, and Judy Holder, elementary school counselor, for offering suggestions; and Eileen Klockars and the wonderful staff at HRD Press for helping to put this book together.

Sharon Scott

AN IMPORTANT NOTE TO PARENTS AND TEACHERS

This book will be more effective for your child or student if you follow these suggestions:

1. First, read the book by yourself. In the process, think about the different values under discussion and any experiences from your life that apply to them. Later, when you read the book with the child, relate some interesting examples of your own.

2. Read the book to or with the child. The comprehension of young children varies greatly, so you may need to elaborate on certain points to help the child understand them. I have "field-tested" this book and found it best for children in grades 2 through 6.

3. Slowly work through the book together, reading no more than one chapter at a time. Engage in some light discussion about what was read. Have the child reflect on what the chapter meant to him or her. Did the chapter make the child want to pursue a project? If so, encourage the child's ideas.

4. Some children may want to draw pictures about what they've read or write a poem or just tell another person about it. Support all of these ideas and more!

5. Avoid lecturing while reading. Don't use this book to discipline the child for failing to exhibit the value discussed (e.g., "This chapter is about honesty. You better pay close attention because of that lie you told me last week"). Do use the book to reinforce a time when the

child exhibited the value discussed (e.g., "Remember how nervous you were when you accidentally broke the neighbor's window playing ball? You told the truth about it. I'm so proud of your honesty!").

6. Chapter 10 presents a series of stories that give the child an opportunity to practice using good values. Each story details a problem and is followed by a solution. Be sure to give the child time to work on the problem before reading the solution.

7. Teaching transparencies and a Nicholas puppet are available to assist educators and other professional helpers in teaching this material. See end section of this book for ordering information.

CHAPTER 1

WHAT ARE VALUES?

Hi! My name is Nicholas.

What Are Values?

Hi! My name is Nicholas. I'm a Cocker Spaniel, and I live in Texas with my mom, my dad, and quite a few animal buddies. My buddies in the house include dogs and cats and a parakeet named Mikey. We live on a farm in the country. Lots of animals live outside in the fields and woods. At night, we hear coyotes howling to one another under the starry skies. Sometimes we see jackrabbits hopping across the pastures with their big ears laid back. Herons and turtles live on our lakes, and the lakes are full of fish. Roadrunners, birds that run on the ground, often cross our path. There are also squirrels, raccoons, skunks, and even armadillos. We don't play with these outside animals. They're wild and free and wouldn't even know how to play with us. We just enjoy watching them.

These animals are smart because they know how to find food, build homes, and raise their families. I'm glad that Mom gives me a nice bed to sleep in and keeps food for me in the kitchen pantry, because I don't think I could do those things without her help! I'm smart in other ways, though. For example, I know how to write books! This is the fifth book I've written. Have you read any of my other books?

Nicholas and Sharon

If you have read my books, then you know that I always write about how to get along with others and make good decisions. My mom, Sharon Scott, is a family counselor, and she helps me a little with my books. When I was trying to decide what this book would be about, she helped me a lot. One day I noticed that she had bought a pretty little pillow and put it in a chair in the family room. She was staring at the pillow, deep in thought. I waited patiently, but she just kept staring. Finally, I asked, "What are you looking at on the pillow?"

Mom said, "Nicholas, look at the words sewn on this pillow. They say, 'My goal in life is to be the kind of person my dog thinks I am.'"

"What does that mean?" I asked.

"Well, it means that you think I'm nice and kind and smart and I want to try to be the best person I can be."

I told Mom that she was the best person in the whole wide world. I told her I thought she was just about perfect!

She smiled and said, "Nicholas, that's one of the nicest things that anyone has ever said to me, but it takes some work to be a good, kind person. It's important to work every day at having good values."

"Values?" I said. "What are values?"

Mom's pillow

Mom replied, "Nicholas, values are hard to explain because they're not anything you can see. I can't show you values. All I can do is tell you about them. Values are qualities of how good and kind people are. Values are the best in people. Values are what people stand for. People who have good values are always fun to be around because they know how to treat others. They're nice. They have good hearts.

"Let's go back to the pillow, because it will help me explain values to you. Remember, the pillow says that my goal is to be like the person you think I am. Well, what kind of person do you think I am?"

"Is this a trick question?" I asked.

"No, Nicholas, this is a serious question. What kind of person do you think I am?"

I told Mom that she was a nice, caring person, someone who was kind, loving, and honest. I added that she was good at laughing and sharing. Since Mom was a volunteer at the Humane Society (which is like an animal shelter), helping to take care of homeless animals, I also mentioned that she was good to animals as well as people.

Mom said, "Nicholas, those are all values. They are the parts of our personality that make us good and kind and nice. You have those good qualities, too. In fact, all animals do. Animals usually solve problems without fighting. People sometimes lose their tempers and find it hard to agree on issues. Animals are usually kind to one another. But sometimes people are rude to one another and call each other bad names. Animals don't tease each other in mean ways, but sometimes people do. Animals don't laugh at you when you make a mistake, but sometimes people do. Animals are honest, but sometimes people are dishonest. Animals don't smoke cigarettes or drink or use drugs—they take care of their bodies. But sometimes people don't take care of their bodies.

"So you see what I'm saying, Nicholas. You have so many good qualities that make you good and kind and nice. They just come to you naturally. That's why people like you so much! As a human, I have to think about values and work hard to have them. Maybe you should write a book that teaches children how to have good values and use them all the time, not just when people are looking. You could explain that it's important to try really hard to be good and kind and nice all the time."

I thought that was a great idea!

So that's how this book got started. Mom and I were just talking about a silly little pillow that had an important message for us all.

Right away, I began thinking about values. I realized there are so many important values in life. We're supposed to be fair, kind, honest, loyal, and trustworthy. We should try to act responsible and show respect. We should accept other people's differences. We should think positive thoughts about others and ourselves. We should mean what we say and say what we mean. Golly, I became so confused, I didn't know where to begin this book!

Mom noticed the confused look on my face and said, "Nicholas, why don't you begin with your name?"

"Huh?" I said.

Mom explained, "I know there are a lot of values to choose from. So just begin with your name. Use the letters of your name—N*I*C*H*O*L*A*S—to list some of the many important values that people should try to have."

And that's when we came up with this list:

<u>N</u> is for nice.

<u>I</u> is for involved.

<u>C</u> is for confident.

<u>H</u> is for honest.

<u>O</u> is for obedient.

<u>L</u> is for loyal.

<u>A</u> is for accountable.

<u>S</u> is for sharing.

And that spells NICHOLAS!

"Mom," I said, "I try very hard to have all of those important values. But I don't want to sound like I'm bragging in my book."

"Maybe you could ask your animal friends about their experiences with those values," she replied.

I liked that idea, and so I decided to ask animals from all over the world to tell their own *true* stories about values. Mom and I got on the computer and e-mailed lots of people asking for stories about animals who showed our special N*I*C*H*O*L*A*S values. We received so many stories that it was difficult to select which ones to put in the book!

In the following chapters, we will learn more from my animal friends and their delightful stories about how to be good and kind and nice. I hope you already have good, strong values. When you finish this book, I hope your values are even stronger!

CHAPTER 2

"N" IS FOR NICE

Jethro

A friend of Mom's, Marc Bekoff, teaches at the University of Colorado in Boulder. He studies animal behavior and writes books about it. He told her this true story about his dog, Jethro. The story is a wonderful example of being *nice*.

Jethro is part German Shepard, part Rottweiler, and maybe a little hound dog. His coat is black and tan, and he has long, floppy ears. He's also a big dog, weighing 90 pounds. Mr. Bekoff met Jethro at the Humane Society many years ago. Jethro was about nine months old at the time. No one knew where Jethro came from or how he came to have no home, but he was excited to get out of the pen and go to live with Mr. Bekoff in his mountain home. Mr. Bekoff soon discovered that Jethro was perfect at helping him study birds in the forest because Jethro was gentle and *nice*.

Jethro and Marc Bekoff

One day, when Jethro was two years old, Mr. Bekoff was sitting inside the house and heard Jethro come to the door. Instead of whining to come inside, as he usually did, Jethro just sat there. Mr. Bekoff looked out the door and noticed a small furry object in the dog's mouth. "Oh, no," he thought, "Jethro killed a bird." But when Mr. Bekoff opened the door, Jethro dropped a tiny baby bunny at his feet!

The bunny was wet from being carried in Jethro's mouth, but she was not injured because Jethro had held her very softly.

Jethro was so proud of himself for finding and saving this helpless baby bunny. Perhaps the bunny's mother had been killed by one of the coyotes, red foxes, or mountain lions that live around Mr. Bekoff's house.

Mr. Bekoff quickly gathered a box, blanket, food, and water for the bunny, who was officially named "Bunny" once she was placed in her box. All this time Jethro watched and whined, wanting to make sure that Mr. Bekoff was careful with the tiny creature. When Mr. Bekoff put mashed-up carrots, celery, and lettuce in Bunny's box, Jethro didn't try to eat the food because he knew it was for the hungry bunny. Jethro refused to leave the box because he was curious about this little ball of fur who was now slowly moving about in her new home.

It was bedtime and Jethro finally had to be dragged away from the box for his nightly walk. As soon as he and Mr. Bekoff returned from the walk, Jethro raced to the box and slept there rather than in his usual bed. Jethro had decided that Bunny was his new friend, and he spent the next few weeks taking great care of her.

Jethro being nice to Bunny

Finally, the day came when Bunny was big enough to go live in the woods with all the other animals. Mr. Bekoff and Jethro walked to the side of their home and released Bunny from her box. They watched as she slowly made her way into a woodpile. She was a little scared, as she had never seen the forest or smelled the big outdoors.

She stayed in the woodpile for about an hour and then confidently stepped out to begin life as a rabbit. Jethro stayed where he had laid down to watch this scene. He never took his eyes off Bunny, nor did he try to approach her. He somehow knew what would make her happy, and that was to be a wild, free rabbit! Every time Jethro was let outside for the next six months, he would always run to the spot where they had let Bunny go. He would turn his head from side to side searching for her. Sometimes they would see Bunny, but Jethro knew that he should not approach her. Jethro was being as *nice* as he knew how to be to his friend Bunny.

Eventually, Bunny grew big and started to look like all the other adult rabbits. Jethro would look at each of them and try to get as close as he could, perhaps trying to decide if it was his good buddy, Bunny.

Bunny in the woodpile

"Wow!" I told Mom. "That Jethro is some dog—he really knows how to be *nice*."

"Yes, he does," said Mom. "But the story doesn't end there."

"What happened next?" I asked.

Mom said that last summer Jethro saved another wild creature's life. Jethro came running up to Mr. Bekoff and dropped a wet bundle at his feet once again. This time it wasn't a bunny, but a young bird—a finch. The little bird had accidentally flown into a window and was stunned. The bird only needed a little time to let its head clear from banging into the glass.

Mr. Bekoff held the finch in his hands for a few minutes while Jethro watched the bird's every move. When the bird seemed stronger, Mr. Bekoff placed it on the railing of his front porch. Jethro walked closer to it, sniffed it, stepped back, and watched it fly away.

Jethro is a hero. He has saved two animals from dying. He could have ignored the helpless creatures. He could have gulped them down in one bite. But instead he chose to be *nice* and make two new friends—if only for a short time.

I told Mom that being a *nice* person was very important. I said, "Mom, could you tell me some things to do to be *nice*? I want to make sure that I'm trying all the time to have this value."

Mom got out her note pad and began listing ways to be *nice:*

Ways to Be Nice

☆ Take turns.

☆ Say only good things about other people.

☆ Don't borrow anything from anyone without asking permission, and remember to say "please."

☆ Don't interrupt when others are talking. Wait until they've finished their sentence before you begin speaking.

☆ When others are saying unkind things about another person, don't join in. Try to change the subject. If that doesn't work, be strong enough to walk away from the conversation.

☆ When someone does something nice for you, always say "Thank you!"

☆ Don't cut in line. Wait your turn.

☆ Never call people any name except their real name. Bullies are uncool.

☆ Don't hit, kick, or shove. Learn to talk out problems.

☆ Try to really care about others—not just yourself.

P.S. Nicholas adds: Always be kind to animals, too! We depend on nice people to care for us!

Mom added that this list could go on and on and on, as there are so many things that we can do to be *nice*. Can you think of other ways to be nice? She said that if you always treat others the way that you want others to treat you, then you are being *nice*.

Mom also said that not only should we be nice to others, but we should be nice to ourselves too. I asked her what that meant. She said that you can be *nice* to yourself by taking care of yourself. For example, eating good foods (including vegetables—which I really like!), exercising, getting plenty of sleep, and getting your homework and chores done on time so that you have time to play and relax. Another *nice* thing to do for yourself is to think positive thoughts about yourself.

Here is a fun assignment. This week do one *nice* thing each day for yourself. Also do one *nice* thing each day for another person—it could be your parent, your teacher, an aunt, a classmate, or a neighbor. But don't tell them what you've done—there's no need to brag. Just do something nice for others!

The "Nice" chart on the next page will help you with this assignment. Keep up your chart for a week or more to get in the habit of being a *nice* person! Then look back at all that you've done to be *nice*, and smile—really big—because it should make you feel proud that you're working hard at being a *nice* person. Just like Jethro is a *nice* dog.

MY "NICE" CHART

On **Monday**, I was nice to myself by _____

On **Monday**, I was nice to _____ by _____

On **Tuesday**, I was nice to myself by _____

On **Tuesday**, I was nice to _____ by _____

On **Wednesday**, I was nice to myself by _____

On **Wednesday**, I was nice to _____ by _____

On **Thursday**, I was nice to myself by _____

On **Thursday**, I was nice to _____ by _____

On **Friday**, I was nice to myself by _____

On **Friday**, I was nice to _____ by _____

On **Saturday**, I was nice to myself by _____

On **Saturday**, I was nice to _____ by _____

On **Sunday**, I was nice to myself by _____

On **Sunday**, I was nice to _____ by _____

Chapter 3

"I" Is for Involved

Trudi

Mom told me about another important value—to be *involved*. Being *involved* is all about reaching out and helping somebody or something. It could be about helping other people, or helping animals, or even helping the environment!

"Nicholas," Mom said, "you've been very good about being *involved*. You've done lots of volunteer work helping people and animals. Do you remember when you were three months old and I began taking you to visit older people in nursing homes? We would go with your brother Shawn. He was older than you and taught you how to act calm and gentle when meeting the people who lived at the nursing home. Many of them were lonely because they didn't have a lot of visitors and weren't well enough to go anyplace on their own."

"Yes, I remember," I told Mom. "In fact, I remember one particular lady who was very old and had long, white hair. She always sat in a wheelchair in the hall outside her room. Before my first visit to the home, you told me about her. You said she had lived in the nursing home for seven years and had never talked. She didn't seem to know what was happening around her. You warned me that she might not even look at me."

I still felt sad just thinking about that.

"But," I continued, "when the three of us walked down the hall, she leaned forward a little and stared at me. We stopped and you started to talk to her like you always did. She kept leaning forward until she was completely bent over looking at me. You told her you had a new puppy for her to see and that his name was Nicholas. You picked me up and put me in her lap. She began stroking my long ears slowly and saying, 'Oh, you pretty thing. You pretty little thing.' Well, the nurses were surprised, as they hadn't heard this lady talk in seven whole years."

"Nicholas, you have such a good memory," Mom said. "You made a difference in that lady's life. You were *involved* in helping her to speak. You've been *involved* in helping so many other times, too. Do you remember when you used to give people a kiss on the nose if they made a donation to help the homeless animals at the Humane Society? You would stand in the booth with me for hours, taking in money to help animals who badly needed good homes. And you've visited many elementary schools, teaching children to be kind to animals. You've always been very *involved*."

"I like being *involved*, Mom!"

"Yes, Nicholas. Being *involved* always makes us feel good inside. And the great thing about helping others is that when we need help, people are willing to help us. By helping us, they feel good inside, too!"

Mom then told me the true story of Trudi, a Boxer dog who can teach us a lot about being *involved*.

Trudi is five years old and lives in Rogers, Arkansas, with her mom and dad, Rozanne and Jack Lovell. Trudi and her dog sister, Fanci, are both registered by Delta Pet Partners. This means that they have been specially trained to visit hospitals, nursing homes, and other places where people are sick or troubled. A Delta Pet Partner dog and its owner have to pass a test in obedience and good disposition. Mrs. Lovell said that Trudi instantly grabbed everyone's heart because she had so much love to give. So both dogs became involved in visiting many places where the kindness of a dog might brighten people's day.

Trudi especially liked older people and visiting nursing homes. She became friends with a lady who was over 80 years old and blind. The lady had few visitors and looked forward to Trudi's visits. Whenever Trudi arrived, the lady would always have a graham cracker waiting for her. The two of them often walked together in the halls of the nursing home for exercise, and the lady always introduced Trudi to any new residents. Trudi even wore special costumes during some of her visits. This gave the residents quite a laugh! Trudi didn't mind wearing a cowboy outfit or doctor outfit, but she didn't like hats—she thought dogs looked silly wearing hats!

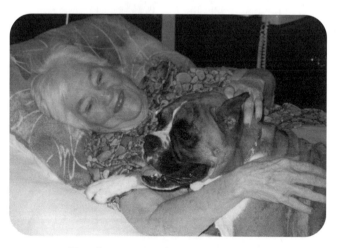

Trudi visiting the nursing home

Trudi also liked children and visiting the children's section at St. Mary's Hospital. One day she met a very ill little girl and stayed with the girl for a long time. When it came time to leave, Trudi had to be pulled away from the bed. Trudi and the girl were told that they could visit more on another day. Trudi knew this girl needed some special love that day. And it made Trudi happy inside to help her.

Trudi and Fanci visited a children's shelter too, a place where children stay if there is a serious problem in their home. Trudi sat with the children, one by one, and listened to them whisper their sad stories in her ear. Their tears fell on her brown coat, but she didn't mind—she was *involved* and knew how important it was to help them.

Trudi involved at the hospital

Trudi and Fanci also helped in the rehabilitation area of St. Mary's Hospital. Some patients there were partially paralyzed because of health problems, and had trouble moving their hands or legs. It was necessary for the patients to practice using those parts of their bodies, and Trudi and Fanci would help them. The physical therapist would give the patients a dog brush so they could exercise by brushing Trudi and Fanci. Sometimes they would play catch with the dogs or shake the dogs' paws.

One day Trudi became seriously ill herself. Her vet couldn't figure out what was wrong with her, so her parents drove her to a big dog hospital in Oklahoma. It had vets called specialists, and they did tests on Trudi. When the test results came back, Trudi's parents learned that her kidneys had never grown correctly in her body. Because of that, her kidneys were failing her. Trudi was a very sick dog.

With proper care and special food, Trudi started to feel a little better. She didn't have the energy she once had, though,

and slept more. Even though she was sick, whenever she saw Mrs. Lovell and Fanci getting ready to make a visit, she was up and ready to go. Trudi was truly *involved!* She wasn't helping others because she was paid to. She wasn't helping because she was made to. And she certainly wasn't helping because she wanted to show off or get attention. She really liked being *involved.* By helping others feel good, Trudi helped herself feel good.

Fanci and Trudi in their costumes

At this point in the story, Mom said, "And, Nicholas, do you know how this story ends? When the residents in the hospital and the nursing home and the children's home learned about Trudi's illness, they made her get-well cards full of sweet wishes. And Trudi was offered a bed to rest in, if she needed it, while visiting those places!"

I thought that was such a great story! A dog decided to be *involved*, and when she needed help, people were *involved* in helping her! I told Mom that I knew how to be *involved* because of the visits that she and I had made to schools and nursing homes. But I wondered how children your age could be *involved* in helping.

Mom said there were so many different ways for kids to help. She told me about a boy named Ocean Robbins who, when he was only seven years old, organized a peace rally at his elementary school. And Danny Seo, at age 12, formed an organization called Earth 2000 with some neighborhood kids. Their goal was to improve the environment. They began by recycling aluminum cans and planting trees. Over the next seven years, their project grew to 20,000 young people, all across the country, who helped in many different ways!

Mom thought for a moment and then pulled out her note pad and started writing down ideas. Her ideas are on the next page. Before you look at them, see if you can come up with some things you could do that would make a difference for somebody or something in your school or neighborhood or even in nature.

Your Ideas

1. _____

2. _____

3. _____

4. _____

5. _____

How Children Can Be Involved!

1. With your family, visit a person in a nursing home once a month. Select someone who gets very few visitors and would really appreciate your visit. Or have your class write letters once a month to residents at nursing homes.

2. Have your school save pennies all year long and then donate them to your local Humane Society to help buy food, toys, blankets, and other items for homeless dogs and cats.

3. Collect aluminum cans in your school cafeteria. Take them to a recycling center and donate the money to a worthy cause.

4. Help Mother Nature by planting a tree in your schoolyard. Think about planting one that has berries that will help feed the birds.

5. When you and your family are thinking about getting an animal friend for your home, adopt one from a shelter. They'll pay you back in love and loyalty the rest of their lives for saving them.

6. If there is someone in your neighborhood who is older and having difficulty doing chores, volunteer to help sweep their driveway, plant spring flowers, or shovel snow from their front porch. Be sure to ask your parents for permission first.

7. Be helpful to nature, and don't harm her little creatures. For example, when a bee flies into your home, realize that he's just made a wrong turn. He doesn't want to hurt you—he just wants to be outside again to get nectar from the flowers and go back to his hive and make honey. So there's no need to scream, yell, and holler! Just open a window or door, and in a minute he'll find his way outside again. Instead of killing such creatures, help them get back to nature. And if someone makes fun of you for being kind, ignore that person. He or she just doesn't know that you're being involved!

8. Plant a small vegetable garden at your house or as a class project. If you have extra vegetables, they could be donated to elderly neighbors.

9. Collect magazines and take them to a nursing home for the residents to read.

10. Think about children less fortunate than you, and try to show you care. You and your classmates could each bring one toy to give to a children's home where children do not have as much as you have. Don't bring an old, broken toy. Bring one of your nice toys and feel good when you give something to help others!

11. Make a birdhouse. Study the type of bird that uses that style of house, and put it in a location where the birds will use it. Birds use their houses in the summer to nest and

in the winter for warm, dry shelter. If you ever find a baby bird on the ground and it has all its feathers, leave it there or set it on a branch. The mother and father birds are nearby and just waiting for you to leave. Don't worry about leaving your scent on their baby by placing it on a branch—most birds don't have a sense of smell. If the baby bird is not feathered, put it back in the nest if you can see the nest and get to it. Or get a basket from your house, set the baby in it, and tie it to the tree where you discovered the baby. The parents will soon find it if you go inside and leave them alone.

12. When you brush your teeth, save water by wetting your toothbrush and then turning the water off. Finish brushing your teeth before you turn the water back on to rinse out your mouth. You'll probably save five or more gallons of water every time you brush!

13. Get a birdbath for your schoolyard or your house. Make sure to put fresh water in it every day.

14. Read to an elderly person who has poor eyesight.

15. When a classmate is ill for several days, call him or her and help with homework over the phone. Before you do this, always tell your teacher what you intend to do, to make sure your teacher thinks it's okay.

16. Pick up litter. It doesn't matter whose it is —help keep your street or playground clean.

17. Have your class be mentors to younger children. A mentor is a helper or a coach to someone who is learning something that the mentor already knows. For example, fourth graders could be mentors to second graders. You could help younger children with their spelling words, reading, and math, or you could just be a big buddy who gives them encouragement. You could teach them how to get along with others, be kind, and, most important, not to gossip or talk unkind about others. You could even read this book to them!

18. When a classmate or a neighbor is sick, make a get-well card and mail it to that person.

CHAPTER 4

"C" IS FOR CONFIDENT

LuckyBoy

"Nicholas," Mom said, "do you know the baseball rule 'three strikes and you're out'? Well, this next story is about a tiny dog who had lots of strikes against him—more than three. He could easily have given up, but he chose not to. He just kept trying! His true tale will remind us how important it is to be *confident* in ourselves."

I asked Mom if being *confident* in ourselves was the same as self-confidence, and she said yes. I then told her, "I always try to believe in myself and in my abilities. I know I'm not good at everything. In fact, I'm poor at some things and only average at others. But there are some areas that I'm really good at."

Mom replied, "Nicholas, what is important is that we all believe in ourselves and trust that we can grow and learn more. Now let me tell you about the tiny dog, LuckyBoy. I recently went to a park and met him and five wonderful people who helped him through hard times. No one knew the whole story until that day in the park, when these five people came together and shared their part of the story. LuckyBoy had to have lots of *confidence* in himself to survive the bad things that happened to him."

Mrs. Seymour, Ms. Dahl, Mr. Seymour,
Mr. and Mrs. Wright with LuckyBoy

Here is what Mom told me.

One sunny day in February, Laura and Brian Seymour were enjoying a walk with their two dogs around White Rock Lake in Dallas, Texas. As they rounded a curve in the jogging trail, they noticed a group of people staring at the water. They also noticed some eight-year-old boys throwing rocks into the water. Curious, they looked toward the lake and came upon a sad sight. A little puppy was stuck in a patch of muddy water full of dead trees and branches. Only the puppy's head was visible—the rest of him was sunk in the mud. The little fellow was trapped and very scared. He didn't understand why no one would help him. He especially didn't understand why the boys would throw rocks at him—he couldn't even run away from them.

Mr. Seymour pulled off his shoes and shirt, and waded into the water and through the mud. He found a big stick and used it to pull the terrified puppy to shore. The puppy was a blonde Chihuahua, and very skinny. Mr. and Mrs. Seymour could see that the puppy's owner had not taken good care of him. They spoke to him kindly, so he would feel less afraid, and set him in the sun to dry off.

Mr. and Mrs. Seymour then noticed something else. They could not believe their eyes! Two other Chihuahua puppies were in the water, and both had drowned. Mr. Seymour and his wife now understood what had happened. The owner of the three puppies had not wanted them and so cruelly took them to the lake to drown them. The rescued puppy had escaped from the owner, only to get stuck in the mud. The mean owner had left the puppy there, thinking that he would die too. The owner didn't know that the puppy would struggle so hard to survive, and not give up. That's a form of being *confident!*

When the Seymours got home, Mrs. Seymour bathed the puppy, to get off all the mud. She put him in a little puppy pen with warm food, fresh water, and a soft blanket. He had been through such an ordeal that he was still scared and cowered in the pen's corner. They named him LuckyBoy because he was a lucky boy—today anyway!

The Seymours cared for the little puppy and liked him a lot, but they already owned two dogs and couldn't keep another one. They called the Richardson Humane Society to see if the people there could find the puppy a good home. This is what the mean owner should have done with the unwanted litter of Chihuahua puppies.

The following weekend, the Richardson Humane Society took the puppy to their Adoption Day. A lady saw LuckyBoy and decided she wanted to take him home. The Society's people told her all about his horrible ordeal, and she promised to love and care for him forever. The lady seemed very nice. Sadly enough, she returned LuckyBoy the next day. "He's not perfect," she said. LuckyBoy, being nervous and scared, had an accident on her carpet. The lady wasn't interested in trying to help him learn better or get over his fear. She just wanted to get rid of him.

LuckyBoy was then adopted by a man who also seemed nice. The man promised to give him a good home and to bring LuckyBoy to a vet for his shots and a check-up. After the man took the puppy home, though, he refused to bring LuckyBoy to a vet. So the Society's people asked him to return LuckyBoy to them. This little 11-pound fur ball deserved a home where he would be fed and cared for properly!

The Richardson Humane Society needed a foster home for LuckyBoy so he could be loved and cared for until they found a really good home for him. Fortunately, in walked Richardson Humane Society board member and "foster mom," Maggie Dahl. She was ready to give LuckyBoy the foster home that he needed.

Her own pets—two beagles, Barcley and Cassie, and three cats, Jasper, Joshua, and Baby—were used to having foster animals at their house, and they loved this extra company. LuckyBoy confused them, though. They couldn't understand why he crouched in the back of the dog carrier and refused to come out.

LuckyBoy's *confidence* was low. He had allowed others to weaken his belief in himself. He had been born with lots of *confidence!* But after being nearly drowned and then rejected twice by people, he wasn't sure about himself anymore. He thought maybe he wasn't worthy of being loved.

Ms. Dahl and her animals proved him wrong! They told LuckyBoy to get his act back together! They reminded him that he had done nothing wrong. He wasn't the one who was mean or unkind—he was good and kind! He just had to believe in himself again. Think positive about yourself, they told him. And LuckyBoy tried—really hard.

At first he clung to Ms. Dahl, but as he began to think good thoughts about himself, the more he felt like playing with her dogs and cats. Before long, he was comfortable playing with them in the house. Having fun outside was the next step. Whenever he ran out to play in the backyard, he'd suddenly get scared and quickly run back inside. But he soon learned to play chase and be brave playing outside. LuckyBoy just needed someone who would give him time and love and be patient with him. Ms. Dahl and her animals gave him exactly what he needed.

One day, LuckyBoy saw a squirrel on the ground eating a pecan. He wanted to play chase with it, and so off he ran. The squirrel saw him coming and quickly ran up a tree. LuckyBoy stopped at the base of the tree, disappointed because, normally, dogs can't climb trees. But then he thought, "Why not try?" And so he tried to run up the tree too!

After this, he kept trying to run up trees as squirrels do, and guess what? One day LuckyBoy took a very long run and landed in the fork of a big tree in Ms. Dahl's backyard.

LuckyBoy had climbed a tree, just like the squirrels! This was an amazing feat. Tiny LuckyBoy, only 16 inches tall, had climbed 60 inches—that's five feet—into the fork of the tree! He believed in himself and was able to do something that most dogs can't do. That's *confidence!*

LuckyBoy showing confidence

Maggie Dahl knew that LuckyBoy was now ready for a permanent home. Every weekend, he went to Adopt-a-Pet hoping for a loving home. He sat so cute in the pen and had *confidence* that someday soon he'd have a home.

Michael and Linda Wright's old Chihuahua, Pancho, had died recently, and they were very sad. They missed their dog so much, but they thought they were finally ready for another dog. They saw LuckyBoy on their computer, at the Richardson Humane Society's web site, and became interested in him. When they saw LuckyBoy in person, they said, "We need each other." LuckyBoy was nervous to be moving again, but soon he was greeted by Mr. and Mrs. Wright's two cats, Maggie and Bucky. In a few days he was settled in. Now he's so at home that he even protects the Wright's property by barking whenever a stranger arrives. He's truly *confident*.

LuckyBoy now has a home

The Wrights decided that LuckyBoy needed a playmate, and so they adopted another dog from the Richardson Humane Society. In fact, LuckyBoy went with them and selected Bert— a cute, shaggy young dog—to be his playmate. LuckyBoy was never able to teach Maggie, the cat, to play chase: she just couldn't get the hang of it. But he was able to teach Bert, and they've been best friends ever since!

Bert himself was abused by humans, and LuckyBoy has helped him become more *confident*. Together, they are learning new things and teaching each other new things. Of course, LuckyBoy is teaching Bert how to chase squirrels!

And, one more thing: LuckyBoy can't climb the trees in the Wright's backyard because they are very tall pines without forks in them. But don't tell LuckyBoy he can't. He runs, jumps, and claws at the trees—and is even able to cling to them for several seconds. LuckyBoy knows he CAN!

LuckyBoy teaches Bert confidence

"Mom, that's so sad about how LuckyBoy's life started out."

"I know, Nicholas, but he had the right attitude—a *confident* one—and his life became better because he didn't give up. And that's what *confidence* is all about—believing in yourself so that you keep trying. Everything may not always work out exactly as we plan it, but if we don't have *confidence*, we simply give up and don't try to make things better and increase our happiness."

"But how do you get *confidence*, Mom, if you don't think you have it?"

"Nicholas, getting *confidence* requires positive thinking. When stinkin' thinkin' comes into your mind, kick it out! You, and only you, control the thoughts inside your head. Stinkin' thinkin' is when you say things to yourself like *'I can't do that,' 'I'm not good at that,' 'I'm too shy to do that,' 'That's too hard to learn,'* or *'I don't want to try that.'* Replace those sentences with positive thoughts:

'I can do that!'

'I'm good at that!'

'I'll try my best!'

'I'm going to have to practice that a lot to learn it.'

'I want to try that.'

"Every time you have *confidence* in yourself and try something new, taste a new food, go out for a new sport, introduce yourself to a new friend, bravely talk in front of your class, or learn something difficult, you build even more *confidence* in yourself!" Just like LuckyBoy built his *confidence*.

CHAPTER 5

"H" IS FOR HONEST

Reilly

"Nicholas," Mom said, "Let's talk about the next important value that people—and animals—should have. That value is *honesty*. *Honesty* is about always telling the truth."

"Why is it important to be *honest?*" I asked.

Mom answered, "Because if you always tell the truth, people know they can trust you and so they believe what you say. If you don't always tell the truth, and lie a lot, then people think twice about trusting you. They never know whether you're telling the truth or not. After a while, they don't believe anything you tell them."

"I want people to believe me, so I always tell the truth. I'm *honest*."

"I know you are, Nicholas, and I'm so proud of you for being *honest*. I want to tell you a true story about a dog named Reilly who is so *honest* that he goes into courtrooms and tells the truth about crimes!"

"You mean Reilly is like a police officer?" I asked.

"You'll find out," Mom replied.

She told me the true story about Reilly, and now I'll tell you!

Reilly, a 10-year-old chocolate-colored Labrador Retriever, jumps up and down as he plays with his yellow tennis ball. Why is Reilly so happy? Because he's a doggie detective who has just helped his human partner, Joe D'Allura, solve another crime!

Reilly is a "scent-discrimination dog." That means he can use his sense of smell to find clues that help people solve crimes. He can even track down the criminal—the person who has committed the crime.

When Reilly was a puppy, Mr. D'Allura noticed that he had the ability to smell and track things really well. So Mr. D'Allura trained Reilly in the search and rescue of lost children and missing persons.

Dogs have a strong sense of smell. It's between 100 thousand to one million times more powerful than a human's sense of smell. Because of this, a dog's nose can detect scents that a person's nose would miss, such as the scent of humans. Human scent is a mix of skin oils, sweat, and dead skin cells—the cells are so tiny, you can't see them. Every person in the world smells different; identical twins even have different scents. Dogs, with their powerful noses, can be trained to tell one person from another, and to search for a person's unique smell.

Reilly can smell a person's scent on the ground, even if that person was there several days ago. He can locate a scent floating on a breeze, floating on the surface of water, or even buried under several feet of dirt. Reilly's nose is so good that he can walk along the top of a deep canyon and tell if the missing person is lost anywhere down below him!

Reilly and Mr. D'Allura

Reilly is also trained to find dead bodies. For example, if a building falls down in an earthquake or a hurricane, Reilly is able to search for the bodies. He has found 10 bodies so far in his lifetime.

Reilly and Mr. D'Allura volunteer about 30 hours a week at the Scent Evidence Canine Unit of the Los Angeles County Sheriff's Department. Sometimes Reilly and Mr. D'Allura are asked to work on special projects for other police agencies and even for the FBI.

Five years ago, Reilly's ability to help the police took a new and even more interesting turn. The Sheriff's Department asked Mr. D'Allura and the other dog handlers to test their dogs' ability to smell human scent on different objects at the scene of a crime.

They soon learned that a person's body will leave skin cells on anything the person touches, no matter how much clothing the person has on, including gloves. As we have learned, skin cells are too small to see, but dogs can smell them!

Reilly getting a scent

"Wow!" I said. "Reilly's nose knows a lot! Does Reilly like to do this work?"

"Yes, Nicholas," Mom replied. "Mr. D'Allura told me that Reilly's always happy when he finds a person or a clue that solves a crime. His reward is playing with his tennis ball—that and kind words from Mr. D'Allura telling him he's done a great job!"

"You said that Reilly is so *honest* that he goes into court-rooms and tells the truth about crimes. Tell me about that, Mom."

"I'll tell you about a case that Reilly recently worked on, one where he helped a police department find the criminal. A 14-year-old boy introduced a friend of his to a drug dealer. Later, the friend met the dealer to buy drugs. The dealer took the money, but drove away without giving the kid any drugs. The kid was really angry about this bad deal. He blamed the 14-year-old boy for introducing him to a drug dealer who could not be trusted."

"Mom, can drug dealers be trusted?" I asked.

"Good question, Nicholas. Kids who get involved in drugs don't seem to think about things like that—the drugs have already scrambled their brains. We have more sense than they do because you and I have never used drugs."

Mom then told me what happened next.

Reilly and his partner are honest

Soon after this bad deal, the 14-year-old boy was in a local park one day with another friend. Someone killed them both. Their bodies were found the next day. There was a huge rock nearby with blood on it. The police investigated the murders and wanted to catch the person who killed these boys. They called in Reilly to help! Using a specially made vacuum cleaner, Mr. D'Allura sucked up scent off the rock. The scent was absorbed by a gauze pad inside the machine.

The police suspected that the kid who lost his money to the drug dealer was still so angry with his friend that he murdered him (and the innocent boy who happened to be with his friend). The kid was brought to the police station and questioned. He admitted that he was at the scene of the murder, but denied he was the killer. After he left the station, Mr. D'Allura used the specially made vacuum cleaner to suck up his scent from the chair on which he had been sitting. Again, the scent was absorbed by a gauze pad inside the machine.

It was now time for Reilly to help! Mr. D'Allura placed a lineup of gauze pads on the floor. The pads were set about five feet apart, and each held a different person's scent. Among them was the pad from the police station, with the scent of the kid who was angry about the drug dealer.

First, Mr. D'Allura had Reilly smell the scent that was taken from the rock at the murder scene; then, he asked Reilly to match that scent with any of the pads on the ground. When Reilly got to the scent of the angry kid, he began jumping around and barking. This was his way of telling Mr. D'Allura that the scents matched. Reilly proved that the kid's scent was on the rock that killed the two boys. Reilly was given his yellow tennis ball and lots of pats for once again helping the police solve a crime.

Other evidence also proved that this kid was the killer. When officers went to his house, they found some blood that matched the blood of one of the boys who was killed. They also found bloody tennis shoes and a wallet in the kitchen trashcan. The wallet belonged to one of the murdered boys.

Mr. D'Allura went to court to testify that Reilly had told him the truth about this case. He showed a video of Reilly doing the scent lineup. The boy was found guilty of murder and will spend the rest of his life in prison. Reilly is truly *honest*.

Mr. D'Allura asking Reilly to match a scent

"Nicholas," Mom said, "Reilly's *honesty* in helping to catch criminals is becoming so well known that seven states now accept scent lineups of trained dogs as evidence in court!"

I told her I was sure that all 50 states would soon realize how valuable trained dogs like Reilly could be in helping to catch criminals.

There are so many good reasons to be *honest* all the time. If you are always *honest*, you will always be believed. Your parents will know that you tell the truth, and they'll be proud of you. For example, if your parents ask you whether you have any homework, and you tell them the truth, they'll think highly of you because you were *honest*.

Your teachers will be proud of you too, because they'll know that *honesty* is an important value to you. Sometimes it may be difficult to tell the truth. For example, if you aren't thinking and get into a fight at recess, you might be tempted to lie about it, to avoid the consequences. But you'll only get in more trouble if you lie! When people aren't *honest*, not only do they get in trouble for what they did wrong, they also get in trouble for lying. So, even when you've made a poor decision or a mistake, it's best to tell the truth about it. Always. You'll get in far less trouble!

Value the truth. Honesty is always best!

CHAPTER 6

"O" Is for Obedient

The swallow family

Mom yelled, "Nicholas, come here! I want you to see something. Hurry!"

I ran into the kitchen as fast as my legs could carry me. Mom was looking out the window at a bird's nest tucked into a corner of our front-porch ceiling. "Watch for the baby birds," she said excitedly. "They're going to leave their nest this morning. It should happen really soon!"

I wondered how Mom could read the minds of the mom and dad birds and know they were going to get their babies to fly out of the nest today. I thought Mom had flipped her wig!

When I asked her how she knew this was going to happen soon, she answered, "I've been watching these birds every summer for the last four years, and they have a routine they follow."

She then told me all about their routine. The birds, called barn swallows, make a nest out of mud and twigs every spring in that corner of our porch ceiling. The parent birds—whom Mom has named Mr. and Mrs. Swallow—usually lay five eggs. Mrs. Swallow sits on the eggs day and night to keep them warm so they will hatch. Mr. Swallow sometimes catches and feeds insects to Mrs. Swallow because he knows she can't leave the nest.

Finally the baby birds hatch—they're very tiny and can't open their eyes at first. Because they don't have feathers yet— just some fuzz—Mrs. Swallow has to keep them warm at night. She does this by carefully sitting on them. During the day, Mr. and Mrs. Swallow keep very busy catching insects to feed their babies. The babies make loud peeping noises when they hear their parents flying toward the nest. Each one is saying, "Feed me—I'm hungry!"

As time goes on, the babies gain weight and finally begin growing beautiful feathers. Then they like to sit on the edge of the mud nest and stretch their wings.

Mom told me this chapter should be about *obedience*. She said that Mr. and Mrs. Swallow talk to their babies and tell them to be careful. They warn the babies not to stretch their wings too wide or wiggle around in the nest at the same time; otherwise, someone could accidentally fall from the nest. The parents tell their babies the rules: to take turns stretching their wings, and not to shove their brothers and sisters in the nest. Mr. and Mrs. Swallow explain to them that by following the rules and minding their parents, they are being *obedient*.

The babies learn that it's important to be *obedient,* and follow the rules, because being *obedient* keeps you safe. If the baby swallows break the rules, what do you think will happen? Someone will fall from the nest, of course. The falling baby could break a leg or a wing and die. Or a cat or a dog could find it on the ground and hurt it.

The swallow babies are obedient

Most boys and girls your age have rules to follow. Here are some of those rules:

- Only talk to people that you know. It can be dangerous to talk to strangers, whether in person or through your computer on the Internet.

- Only have company over when your parents are home and you have their permission.

- Sit properly in your place—if you stand on chairs or tables, you could hurt yourself.

- Put your bicycle and toys away where they belong when you're through with them so people don't fall over them.

- Always make sure your parents know where you are.

- Walk quietly in the halls at school.

- Only go swimming when you are with an adult who knows how to swim.

- Always wear your seat belt when you're riding in the car.

- When you want to pet a dog or a cat that isn't yours, always ask permission from the owner first.

- Listen in school when your teacher, class-mates, or others are talking and sharing.

There are so many rules to follow! And there are reasons for all of them! They help to keep us safe and bring order to our homes and classrooms. So being *obedient* is a good thing because it helps to protect us.

Not too long after I learned all this from Mom, she pointed out something special outside the window. "Look, Nicholas!" she said. "The swallows asked their swallow relatives to come watch the babies fly from their nest. See how many adult birds are flying around to support the babies on this very important day in their lives."

Then we both watched as Mr. and Mrs. Swallow took turns hovering in front of the nest, showing and telling their babies how to flap their wings. They were telling the babies to follow the rules—to be *obedient*—so they would be able to fly and would be safe.

Soon, one by one, four babies flew from the nest and soared in the wind with their parents and other relatives. They chirped and sang all day as they practiced flying, diving, and trying to catch fast-moving insects. A fifth baby sat on the edge of the nest and practiced flapping her wings. She was too scared to try to fly. She was probably the last one to hatch and so was a little smaller than the rest.

Mrs. Swallow telling her babies to follow rules

That night, we watched Mr. and Mrs. Swallow come and go from a porch ledge next to the nest. They were hard at work feeding their babies dinner. They knew the babies had not caught enough insects on their own to fill their stomachs. The smallest baby sat in the nest knowing that tomorrow would be her day to soar. She knew the rules and knew she could do it!

The next day dawned sunny and warm. When Mom and I got up to check the bird's nest, we saw no baby in it. We looked out across the yard and saw seven swallows happily in flight! All the babies had learned to fly and now were on their way to being grown-up birds. They had been safe and successful at learning to fly because they had followed their parents' rules and been *obedient*.

For the next week, the babies slept on the ledge with their parents. Each day their parents had to feed them less and less because they were so good at catching their own meal of bugs.

"Look, Nicholas," said Mom. "Only Mr. and Mrs. Swallow are on the ledge tonight. Their babies have grown up and left home to live lives of their own. The parents taught their babies the rules. And the babies were smart enough to know that being *obedient* would help them grow up."

The babies mind their parents by
sitting on the ledge

"Nicholas," Mom added, "do you remember when you were a puppy and I taught you some rules?"

"Yes, I do. You taught me to go to the bathroom outside in the grass and to be polite and not jump on people when they visit. You taught me a lot of things."

"And, Nicholas, you were *obedient*. That's one reason why you grew up to be such a great dog. You followed the rules, and so there was order and peace in our home. You even went to school and learned to *obey* me when I call you or I ask you to sit or lie down. I was happy because I knew *obedience* would help to keep you safe. That's why parents and teachers give rules and ask us to be *obedient*. They know that minding the rules helps to keep us safe. It also brings order to our homes and classrooms."

Think about how well you follow the rules at school and at home. If your teacher puts your name on the chalkboard a lot or sends you to the principal's office all the time, then you're not being *obedient* these days. If your parents fuss at you a lot or cut back on privileges all the time, then you're probably not being *obedient* there.

Right now you may be thinking about other kids who don't always follow the rules. Perhaps they're your classmates or your brothers or sisters. And you may want to talk about how those kids aren't *obedient*. If you're thinking that way, please stop now! Quit doing it—this is about you! Not someone else! Think about what you can do to be more *obedient*. Are there certain rules you have trouble following? Decide to work harder at *obeying* those rules. Pick one rule right now and start working harder to follow it. Be your best! I know you can be!

What rule will you work harder to follow?

Rule: _____

_____

_____

CHAPTER 7

"L" IS FOR LOYAL

Jiggs

Mom said, "Nicholas, dogs are known for being *loyal*. They stick by your side in good times or bad! They love you, no matter what. Dogs don't gossip about people. Dogs never ever criticize! If you're lonely, a dog will sit by your side. You can tell a dog all your secrets, and the dog will never tell anyone else. When you're sad, dogs will often bring you a toy to try to make you laugh. You dogs are great because you are so *loyal*. And *loyalty* is the value that this chapter is going to be about.

"You're going to laugh when you hear this story, Nicholas, because it's not about a dog being *loyal,* but about a turtle being *loyal!* In fact, a turtle who's been *loyal* for over 66 years!"

"A turtle?" I said. "Turtles can be *loyal?*"

"This one is! His name is Jiggs. You've got to hear his story! You won't believe it, but it's true! The story was on the front page of our newspaper, *The Dallas Morning News,* on June 23, 1999."

Here is what I learned about Jiggs, the *loyal* turtle.

Sixty-six years ago, Ken Connor was five years old and living in Hawthorne, California, with his family. One day he was playing in a neighbor's backyard and spotted a young brown-and-black desert tortoise walking through the grass. He decided to take him home and let him live in his backyard. He hoped the turtle would stay there. He named the turtle Jiggs after a character in a comic strip and painted the name on the turtle's shell. That was in 1933.

Mom interrupted the story to tell me that Ken was young and didn't know that it's dangerous to paint a turtle's shell because the paint can kill the turtle. She also told me that, today, there are laws that forbid taking a desert tortoise out of its natural environment without a permit. I was glad Mom added that information, because we don't want to hurt animals or break any laws.

Fortunately, Jiggs survived the paint—probably because Ken hadn't used much of it—and loved living in Ken's backyard. Ken and Jiggs became best buddies and grew up together. When Jiggs was fully grown, he weighed about 15 pounds.

One day, when Ken was a young man of about 18, Jiggs disappeared from the yard. Ken had no idea where Jiggs went and missed his old friend.

Two years later, Jiggs showed up in the yard—with his name still on his back! Ken had no idea where the turtle had been. He didn't care. Jiggs was home again, and Ken was so happy to have his special friend back. That was in 1948.

The years have flown by, and now Mr. Connor lives in a nursing home. And Jiggs, who's now old too, is there as well. The home has an enclosed courtyard, and that has become Jiggs' playground. Jiggs loves to walk around munching on grass and walking among the flowers. Jiggs has a little doghouse for shelter and a bowl for food and water. His favorite food is purple seedless grapes, and he wags his stumpy tail and squeaks while eating them!

When Jiggs wants to come inside, he scratches at the door. He usually heads for Mr. Connor's room, but on the way, he might stop at the TV room or exercise room to visit with people there. He doesn't like storms and always comes inside then.

Mr. Connor often picks up his friend and tells him, "Hey, kid. Hey, Jiggsie. We've been friends for a long time. Friends for life."

Mom said, "Nicholas, isn't that a fabulous story about *loyalty?* Mr. Connor and Jiggs have been friends for 66 years!"

The Dallas Morning News: Richard Michael Pruitt

Jiggs was loyal to Mr. Connor

"Nicholas," Mom said, "there are many ways to practice the value of *loyalty*. You can be *loyal* to people. For example, when you have an argument with a family member or a friend, try to talk it out. Don't just drop them from your life. Support your family and friends when they need your help. Encourage them to be their best. And don't be jealous of them when good things happen to them. In fact, be proud of them. That's being *loyal*.

"You also can be *loyal* to your country. For example, you can sing the national anthem and be proud of the freedom for which it stands. Some men and women protect our country by serving in the Army, Navy, Marines, or Air Force. They are being *loyal* to their country.

"Husbands and wives can, and should be, *loyal* to each other. They should love, honor, and respect each other. That's the commitment they made when they got married."

I added, "Don't forget, Mom, Jiggs taught us that dogs and cats and other animals—even turtles—can be *loyal* to people. And our humans can be *loyal* to us by taking good care of us for our entire life!"

CHAPTER 8

"A" IS FOR ACCOUNTABLE

Loco

"Nicholas," Mom said, "I recently visited with a little dog named Loco in Dallas, Texas. He weighs only 18 pounds and is part-Beagle and part-Dachshund. This little dog has many important lessons to teach us, especially about the value of being *accountable*."

I asked Mom what the word *accountable* means, because it's a pretty big word. She told me it's a pretty big value!

She said, "Nicholas, being *accountable* is the same thing as being responsible. It's about doing what's really right. Sometimes what we want to do is different from what we should do."

I understood that because I'd like to eat ice cream all the time, but I know that's not being responsible, or *accountable*. It's important to take care of my body and eat good food.

I asked her about her meeting with Loco the dog. This is his true story. It's a sad story, but it has a happy ending.

The little dog's life started off tough. His owners didn't want him, and instead of finding another home for him, they simply left him at the side of a highway in San Antonio, Texas. He was only four months old. He was sure that his owners would return, and so he just sat there and waited and waited. He watched every car that drove by, looking for them. Finally, Nery Garoz, a truck driver, drove by, saw the poor pup, and stopped to pick him up.

Mr. Garoz took the dog home with him, to Dallas. His daughter and her husband, Carol and Greg Autry, live next door to him, and when they saw the little dog, they fell in love with him. They became his new owners and named him Lucky.

The little dog was so happy to have a good home! When he would come in from playing outside, he would take a giant leap into the lap of whoever was sitting on the couch and give that person lots of kisses. He was so funny that the Autrys decided to change his name to Loco, which means "crazy" in Spanish.

Loco had it made! He had a family who loved him, including the Autry's other two dogs, Pooch and Muñeco. And because his grandparents, Mr. Garoz and his wife, were right next door, he could play in their yard as well as his own. Both yards were safely fenced and there was an opening between them. Loco, Pooch, and Muñeco had lots of space for running around and playing!

Loco with Mr. and Mrs. Autry

One day, in January 2001, Loco's life took a difficult turn. The Autrys came home and didn't see Loco in their backyard. They thought he was in his grandparents' backyard, but soon discovered that Loco had disappeared. There was no way out of the fenced yards. Somebody must have reached over the fence and taken him.

The Autrys searched the neighborhood calling his name. They put up flyers asking for his safe return. But Loco was gone. They were so sad.

Four days later, Mr. Autry arrived home from work and saw Loco sitting on the front porch! He was so excited. As he ran to Loco, he noticed that Loco's head was hanging very low. When he reached the little dog, he saw dried blood all over Loco's eyes. One eye was tightly closed and the other was badly swollen. Loco looked hungry and thirsty too, as if he'd had no food or water since his disappearance. Loco was in a lot of pain.

Mr. Autry rushed Loco to the vet. After the vet examined Loco, she told Mr. Autry that Loco was blind in both eyes and that she could tell someone had blinded him on purpose. Mr. Autry was shocked. He couldn't believe it—why would somebody be so cruel? There was no reason—whoever had hurt Loco was very ill and needed help right away.

The Autrys decided they had to warn people that there was a very sick person in the community. They didn't want this to happen again. They wanted to protect children and animals. They wanted this person caught so that the person could get help.

The Autrys notified the press, and stories about Loco's tragedy appeared on the TV news and in the newspapers. People began donating money to the vet to help with the expense of Loco's surgery. School children sent Loco get-well cards. Everyone felt so sorry for Loco. Both eyes had to be removed and then the eyelids stitched shut.

Mom said, "Nicholas, the story could end here with Loco blind and sitting at home feeling sorry for himself. Mr. and Mrs. Autry could be scared and angry and do nothing but talk about how horrible some people are. But the story doesn't end here."

I asked her what happened next, and she told me.

When Loco came home after the surgery, he sniffed the air and wagged his tail happily. He knew that he was home! He greeted his best buddy, Pooch—an old fellow who can only see out of one eye himself. Then Loco ran around the edges of every room in the house. He wanted to re-learn, by smell and touch, the location of everything. He was determined to keep on living as a happy dog.

A reporter at this happy homecoming spoke with the Autrys about the law in Texas for being cruel to animals. You see, cruelty to animals is a crime. The Autrys were shocked to learn that someone found guilty of hurting animals could be sentenced to only a year in jail and, at most, have to pay a $4,000 fine! The Autrys were angry that the punishment for such a horrible act could be so small. That certainly wasn't right! They also believed strongly that anyone found guilty of such a crime should have to get counseling help too.

Mrs. Autry began a petition that called for two important changes in the Texas law: a stronger penalty for cruelty to animals, and required counseling for anyone who has committed such a horrible crime.

Loco and his family got involved

A few days later, Mr. Autry searched the Internet for information on this subject—and found something exciting! Just the day before, at the Texas Capitol, Representative Manny Najera had introduced House Bill 653 to increase the penalties for cruelty to animals. Mr. Autry called Representative Najera's office and asked how he and his wife could help support the bill. He was told to keep the petition going. Eventually, 27,000 people signed it! Then Senator David Cain introduced the bill into the Texas Senate.

To make a long story short, House Bill 653 was made a new law. Now if anyone in Texas is found guilty of being cruel to an animal, he or she can be put in state prison for two years and fined $10,000! Loco was blinded, but thanks to his courage and the Autry's *accountability*, the Texas legislature was able to see the light!

I told Mom that was a fantastic story of how people and dogs can make good things happen when they're determined and try hard.

Mom said, "Nicholas, here's the best part!"

Because the Autrys and Loco had been such a big help in getting people to support the bill, they were invited to a special ceremony in June at the Operation Kindness Animal Shelter. There, Loco sat next to the Governor of Texas, Rick Perry, and paw-printed the bill into law! Everyone was so proud when Loco had his little foot placed in ink so that he could sign the bill. Applause burst out among the crowd of onlookers!

This is probably the only time that a dog signed a piece of legislation into law!

Loco and Governor Perry sign the new law

Since then the Autrys and Loco have visited schools, hospitals, and animal shelters, teaching people about giving kindness to every living creature.

The Autrys state: "We feel it is our calling to educate children and adults about animal cruelty. If it's not stopped, then the person often will become cruel to people as well. We also feel that because of the outpouring of kindness from people all over Texas and the United States, we should give back that kindness to the people who helped us through a tragic time in our lives. Our only regret is that the person who committed this act has not yet been caught. It's not that we want so much to punish, but to get the person help. You see, the experts tell us that a young person most likely committed this act. A young person who is undergoing some sort of abuse him- or herself. This person needs help. Loco has taught us so much . . . forgiveness, overcoming hard times, and hope. All of these things we were reminded of by a little 18-pound dog!"

The Autrys and Loco were honored by Operation Kindness with the 2001 Sarah M. and Charles Seay Kindness to Animals Award.

Loco's family with the
Kindness to Animal Award

Mom said, "Nicholas, do you remember what value this chapter is teaching us?"

"Yes, the value of being *accountable*. And that's exactly what Mr. and Mrs. Autry were. They did what was right. They didn't sit home and complain about how the law should be—they took action and helped to change the law to what it should be. That was being *accountable*.

"But, Mom, how do children reading this book be *accountable*?"

She pulled out her note pad again, and here's what she wrote:

How To Be Accountable

✓ Always tell the truth.

✓ When you've made a mistake, say you did and then apologize.

✓ Stop making excuses for yourself. Be responsible.

✓ Keep your promises. When you say that you're going to do something, do it.

✓ When a person is picking on someone, tell that person to stop being mean. Take up for people when they need help. Bullies are not cool, and people need to tell them that.

✓ When you see something that's wrong, figure out how you can make it better and then do it.

I added, "Mom, people should always be *accountable* to us animals as well. When they bring us into their homes, they should give us food and clean water, and love us every day. They should play with us and give us attention. They should not let us have babies. There are already too many animals in the world who don't have homes. We depend upon people to take good care of us."

"One other thing, Nicholas," Mom said. "If children ever feel so bad that they start thinking about hurting a person or an animal, they should turn to a trusted adult and talk about how sad or angry they feel. The adult should be able to help them.

"Remember: a person who has been hurt by others will sometimes feel like hurting someone or something weaker— such as a young child or an animal. That is not right. And that is not a way to get help or feel better. It's only a way to feel worse. So it's very important to talk to someone we trust any time we need help."

CHAPTER 9

"S" IS FOR SHARING

Cain

"Nicholas, the next value is about *sharing*. You've always been so good at this value. We have lots of other animals living in our home, and all of you get along so well. No one worries that someone else is getting more attention or more food or more time with me, and everyone does a great job of taking turns. All of you are good at sharing toys, too—everyone knows that when you let others play with your toys, they don't mind letting you play with theirs. Sharing helps all of you get along with each other. And it makes me happy watching the whole bunch of you!"

"But, Mom, it's sometimes hard to share when I've just been given a brand-new toy. Sometimes I have to remind myself that my brothers and sisters aren't going to break the toy and just want to look at it."

"What's important, Nicholas, is that when we want to see or borrow something from another person, we always ask permission first. That let's the other person know that we respect his or her property. And the person has a choice of whether to let us *share* or not. And it is that person's choice.

"Nicholas, I now want to tell a delightful, true story about Cain, a boy dog who became a mama cat! He knows a lot about *sharing*. I recently met Cain, and his mom told me this story and showed me pictures to prove it!"

Read on for the story about Cain and real *sharing*.

One spring day, Alison Reynolds opened her apartment door. To her surprise, a six-month-old shaggy blonde puppy walked right in! He was lost. Alison ran ads in the newspapers, trying to find his home. But no one answered the ads. None of her neighbors had seen the dog before, either. So here he was, needing a home.

Alison named the dog Cain and called her mother for help. Alison's mother, Sandi Reynolds, is a former president of the Denton Humane Society. Even though Mrs. Reynolds already had two other dogs and 13 cats, she agreed to take Cain. She figured, "What's one more to love?"

Life was good for Cain. Mrs. Reynolds also had a great big Shepherd-Chow-mix dog named Cypress. Cypress became Cain's best friend.

Cain and Mrs. Reynolds

Mrs. Reynolds fosters kittens for the Humane Society. This means that she takes care of kittens until they are old enough to move to a good home. Kittens need close attention and care until they're six to eight weeks old. After that, they're able to live on their own with a family. So Cain was used to seeing kittens come and go a lot. He usually just ignored them.

When Cain was about one year old, Mrs. Reynolds brought home two "bottle babies" to take care of. "Bottle babies" are kittens so very young that they have to be given a bottle of kitten formula every few hours. The two babies that Mrs. Reynolds brought home were only a week old and so tiny that their eyes were still closed. An old building had been destroyed and their mother had been inside and accidentally killed. Construction workers found the tiny babies and got them to Mrs. Reynolds to try to save their lives.

As Mrs. Reynolds fed the baby kittens, she noticed that Cain was acting very interested. She thought that he wanted to drink their milk! However, when the milk was gone, he was still acting interested and kept staring at the babies. Mrs. Reynolds held one down for him to see better. Cain began gently licking the tiny kitten and cleaned it all over. He then did the same thing with the other kitten.

Cain shares with the kitten

Cain had seen many kittens before, but these were the first ones in which he had shown any interest. Apparently they were so tiny and in such great need that he thought he should help them. He decided to become their mama! Cain even let the kittens try to nurse on him. Boy dogs don't give milk like mama cats do, but Cain and the kittens didn't seem to know that. When the kittens got older, he played with them. When they would wander out of the living room, he would bring them back to safety by walking in front of them and telling them to follow him.

The kittens were finally weaned, which means they could eat kitten food on their own. When they were eight weeks old, both kittens were adopted into good homes. Cain became very sad because he missed his "babies."

Soon, though, another litter of "bottle babies" arrived. There were five of them this time, and they were only two days old. Kittens this young without a mother often die. Mrs. Reynolds said she would not have taken all five in had it not been for the help she knew Cain would give her in caring for them. All five of them lived! In fact, one went to the home of Alison Reynolds, the daughter who had found Cain.

"Nicholas," Mom said, "when I met with Mrs. Reynolds and Cain, she told me that Cain has *shared* his life with about 20 kittens! They're all alive because he knew the importance of *sharing!*"

Cain and kitten napping

I thought that was an amazing story! I asked Mom how we can all learn to *share* and put this value into practice. Presto!—she pulled out her note pad again. Here's what she wrote:

How Do You Share?

1. Share yourself by being a good friend. Listen and talk with lots of people—not just your best friend. You can have more than one friend! And don't act stuck up—like you think you're better than others.

2. Share some things that you own with friends who will carefully play with them. For example, let others play with your games. Take turns.

3. Share your knowledge. If someone is having trouble learning something that you happen to be good at, then help him or her to learn it.

4. Share your home with people. Always make others feel welcome when they visit you. Offer them refreshments. Have fun ideas of things to do while they are visiting.

5. Share your joy. Talk about the good things that are happening in your life. Quit whining and complaining about things. Be positive!

6. Share your laughter. Give lots of smiles to others and laugh often!

Chapter 10

Let's Practice!

LIGHTS . . .
CAMERA . . .
ACTION!

Mom and I practice at a school

"Mom," I said. "These stories have taught me so much about so many important values."

"And, Nicholas," Mom replied, "we heard even more stories about animals who can help teach us about good values! We aren't able to put all of them in the book, because then the book will be too long. But we should mention a few especially interesting ones.

"We heard from a friend of ours, Deb Stover, from Dallas, who wants everyone to know about the *loyalty* shown by her dog, a black Giant Schnauzer named Libby. Libby saved Ms. Stover's life by waking her up in the middle of the night to tell her that the house was on fire. We also heard from Carole Gold of Las Vegas, Nevada, who told us about her *loyal* Keeshond dog, J.D. One day he came in from the patio and started barking and acting 'weird' around her. He kept this up until she finally got the message and went out on the patio. There she found that the hose to the gas grill had come unhooked and dangerous gas fumes were leaking. J.D. saved their lives!"

"Those are serious stories, Mom," I said. "I think the funniest story we heard was about a family of baby ducks who fell down a sewer grate in Canada. The mother duck was *accountable* because she acted when she saw that something was wrong. A police officer was walking nearby, and she went right up to him and kept grabbing at his leg. Then she waddled to the sewer grate, where she sat and waited for the officer to investigate. When he went up to her and looked in the grate, he saw eight tiny babies in the water below. They had slipped through the grate when they were walking with their mama. The officer called a tow truck to remove the grate and lifted the babies out to safety. The mama duck and the babies then left for a nearby pond!"

"That's a darling story, Nicholas," Mom said. "Debbie Winters, who lives in Dallas, also told us a great story. She's a diabetic, and her black-and-white cat, Beauregard, shows *involvement* by paying attention to her blood-sugar levels. Somehow he can tell when her blood sugar drops too low! When it does, he alerts her to this health emergency so she knows to test her blood and quickly take care of the problem.

"Ms. Winters also told us about a 38-year-old horse named Big Boy who one day refused to go into his stall at feeding time. He stayed out in the pasture with another, smaller horse named April. Ms. Winters kept calling him and finally he backed up so she could see April better. April's hoof was caught in the fence and she needed help. He also showed the value of *involvement*."

Mom added, "We heard about so many dogs who are *nice* and show *involvement* by visiting schools or nursing homes. One of them is Mickey, a Cocker Spaniel adopted by Kathi Alexander, who lives in Maryland. Another is a huge Saint Bernard named Edison. His mom, Connie Vollrath, from Arizona, tells us that he is a gentle giant on his visits."

"And, Mom, don't forget Rosie and Daisy—two Coonhound dogs who were adopted by Cindy Lewis, who lives in Arizona. They're sisters and were ill and helpless when Mrs. Lewis took them in. Later, they turned around and were *accountable* by helping to save the lives of her other two dogs, Rocky and Rags. The two dogs had gotten into a fight with a porcupine, and their faces were covered with painful quills. Even though Rocky and Rags were more than a quarter of a mile from their house, somehow Rosie and Daisy knew that they were injured. The sisters were able to tell Mrs. Lewis that their buddies were in danger and needed help fast!"

Mom thought it was amazing how Rosie and Daisy knew something bad was happening so far from their house. She went on to remind me about another amazing story.

"Bonnie Dockery of Rowlett, Texas, told us that over the years she has taken in 24 abused or injured cats, nursed them back to health, and tried to find homes for them. The cats are always frightened when they arrive at her house, but it's been easier for them since one of her cats, Harley, decided to help out. He became a 'Welcome Ambassador' and now does his best to comfort new arrivals. He greets the cats with a 'meow' and then sits quietly with them for as long as it takes for them to calm down. When he feels they've accepted their new home, he gives them a 'welcome bath' by licking them! He then goes about his business, making sure all the other cats are getting along. Harley is truly a peacemaker, and he demonstrates the value of being *nice*."

"Mom," I said, "putting good values into practice often seems to require some sort of decision. We can do one thing, or do another. For example, Harley could have been jealous of the other cats, but instead he decided to show good values and be *nice*."

"That's right, Nicholas. And sometimes we're in situations that make the decision a little difficult. Let me tell you some stories about children in situations like that. They have to decide what to do, and could show good values or not."

Read on and think about how you would handle these situations!

Scooter's Story

J.J. was a new student in Mrs. Smith's third grade class. He had just moved to the United States from Mexico. That day at recess the kids learned that J.J. had never played softball before. Everytime someone threw the ball to him, he dropped it, and he couldn't hit when he was up to bat. A few of the kids started to talk about how lousy he was at softball. J.J. told them that at his old school, all the kids played soccer. No one wanted J.J. on his team.

The next day, a popular boy nicknamed Scooter became captain of one of the softball teams. As he began to select members for his team, a boy behind him whispered, "Scooter, please don't pick J.J. for our team. We won't have a chance of winning with him on our side."

Scooter had just read this book in school and wanted to be a *nice* person. What do you think he should do?

Scooter Decides to Be *Nice*

Scooter thought about J.J.'s feelings—it would hurt to be picked last for a team all the time. He also knew that if the kids allowed J.J. to play the game, J.J. would eventually become better at it. Scooter knew, too, that winning wasn't the most important thing in life—and that acting *nice* was.

Scooter told the other boys: "Since J.J. is a new student, I'm going to pick him first. We want to help him become a really good softball player. So our side is going to show him some things that will help him get better at softball. And I've always wanted to learn how to play soccer. So I suggest that tomorrow we ask J.J. to teach us the game that he plays well. Are you guys up to learning something new?"

Most of the boys yelled, "Yeah, sounds like fun!"

J.J. had a big smile on his face as he walked over and stood next to Scooter. He was so happy that Scooter had included him. And Scooter smiled too, because it always feels good when we're *nice*.

Sasha's Story

One day after school, Sasha was getting into her mother's car and noticed lots of litter in the school's front yard. She also noticed that her redbrick school building did not really look very pretty. The flowerbeds next to the front door had no plants in them. She wondered why no one had tried to clean up the school.

Later, when her mother turned onto their street, Sasha noticed their neighbor, an elderly lady, leaning on a broom in her driveway. The lady was trying to rake leaves and looked really tired. Sasha wondered if the lady had any grown children to help her.

When they got home, Sasha's mother fixed her a snack. As Sasha sat at the kitchen table, she noticed a dog running outside. The dog would run one way and then the other—he looked lost. Sasha couldn't believe that the owner would let the dog run loose. Someone needed to help this dog.

Sasha has a lot of things on her mind. What do you think she should do?

Sasha Decides to Be *Involved*

It became clear to Sasha that she was the one who had noticed these things in need of attention. Who better to get *involved* but her?

She immediately told her mother about the lost dog, and they both rushed out to help him. Sasha's mother warned her that he might not be friendly, so they approached him carefully. The dog was friendly, and ran to them, wagging his tail. They saw that he was wearing a collar with a tag. On the tag was a phone number! After they put him in the backyard and gave him some food and water, they called the number. A woman answered the phone and, hearing about the dog, happily shouted, "They've found Pander! And he's all right!" It turned out that during a storm two nights before, the wind had blown down a section of her fence. Her family had been searching for their much-loved dog ever since.

Next, Sasha went across the street and asked the elderly neighbor if she could help with the raking. The lady, who had always liked Sasha, seemed very grateful and insisted on giving her a dollar for helping.

The next day at school, Sasha asked her teacher if she could talk to the class about the school's appearance. The class got excited about a clean-up project. They decided to form litter patrols at recess, to help keep trash picked up. They called these patrols "The Clean Machine." Then they made posters with the message "Keep Our School Clean!" and put them around the school to remind everyone not to litter. Sasha also suggested that the students raise money to put toward buying flowers for the school's entrance. They could do some extra chores for their parents or a neighbor and ask for a dollar. The students liked her suggestion. Sasha donated the dollar that she had earned, to start the project. With the money they earned, the students planted blue pansies and rosemary shrubs. The school looked beautiful!

Sasha was so proud of herself for deciding to become *involved*. And she couldn't believe how much difference it made in so many people's lives, including her own.

Emma Jane's Story

Emma Jane was a good student. She spoke softly when she talked and sometimes would take a little long to start speaking. When asked a question, she always thought carefully before answering. Because of this, people often talked for her—not only adults, but kids too. And they would say to others, "Emma Jane is shy." She really didn't like that label, but she didn't know what to do about it.

One day Emma Jane noticed that another girl in her class was quiet too. She didn't know the girl very well, though.

Emma Jane wanted people to stop calling her shy. And she didn't want to feel shy either. What do you think she should do about this?

Emma Jane Decides to Be *Confident*

Emma Jane decided to work on being more confident about herself. She asked the other girl, Mandy, if she would like to practice speaking louder so that people wouldn't keep calling them shy. Mandy thought that was a good idea.

They got their parents' permission to get together every weekend, and then used the time to practice reading out loud to each other. They made sure they spoke in a clear, strong voice and talked louder than usual. They both asked their parents to please stop calling them shy. They explained to their parents that it made them feel uncomfortable.

At school, if someone began answering for them before they had a chance to speak, they politely would say, "Thank you for trying to help. But please give me just a second. I want to speak for myself." Then they would talk for themselves, using the louder voice they had practiced. It wasn't always easy, but they kept trying. And they kept getting better.

They acted *confident* in themselves before they actually felt that way. And soon they really did feel *confident!* They knew they could do whatever they wanted as long as they believed in themselves!

Bill's Story

Bill was sitting at the kitchen table finishing his homework. He was bored, so he called his dog, Pudgie, over to play. Pudgie grabbed his favorite plaything—a tennis ball—and brought it to Bill. The boy decided to play catch with Pudgie, and threw the ball for Pudgie to chase. Bill knew he wasn't supposed to play catch in the house, because it's really an outdoor game. Pudgie got excited and started barking. Bill threw the ball farther this time.

That's when it happened. The ball hit a lamp in the den, and the lamp fell to the floor and broke into many pieces. About that time Bill's dad walked in from the garage. He saw the broken lamp, the tennis ball, and Pudgie standing near the lamp.

Bill's father asked, "What in the world happened?"

What do you think Bill should say to his father?

Bill Decides to Be *Honest*

Bill could have blamed the broken lamp on his dog. But he knew that blaming Pudgie would not be right—Pudgie would get in trouble for something he did not do. Bill knew that if he lied, he would feel guilty and have trouble sleeping. He also knew that if somehow his dad found out that he was lying, he would get in even more trouble. So Bill decided it was best to be *honest*.

Bill said, "Dad, I know I wasn't supposed to throw Pudgie's ball in the house. I'm sorry that I did, and I won't do it again. I'll pay for the lamp by doing extra chores."

Bill's father replied, "Bill, I appreciate your offer to pay for the lamp that you broke. We'll work out an extra chore schedule after you finish your homework. No TV for two nights for not following the rules."

Bill felt good about being *honest*. It's the only way to be!

Cody's Story

Cody had just gone to bed and was almost asleep when he heard his mother yell, "Fire! Everyone get out of the house fast!" Cody jumped out of bed and noticed that smoke was already filling his room.

His family had once conducted a fire drill in their home, and his parents had told him to go out the side door of his room if there was ever a fire. He then was supposed to meet his brothers and sisters by the mailbox in the front yard.

But now Cody wasn't completely sure what to do. He was worried about his mother. Her shouts had come from the front of the house. He wondered how he should act. Should he try to run down the smoke-filled hall to get to her, or should he get out the side door?

What do you think Cody should do?

Cody Decides to Be *Obedient*

Cody quickly decided that he should follow the plan his parents had made during the family's fire drill. He quickly dropped to the floor to get below the smoke, and crawled to the side door of his room. He quickly got out and ran to the mailbox in the front yard. He found all of his family gathered there.

About that time, the house exploded. The firemen arrived and put the fire out. They discovered that the cause of the fire was a gas leak.

By being *obedient* and following the rules, Cody had actually saved his own life!

Maggie's Story

Maggie was in the fourth grade. Her teacher told the class that there would be a new student arriving tomorrow. The teacher wanted the whole class to make the newcomer feel welcome.

The next day, when the new student arrived, Maggie was surprised. The student was an old friend of hers named Shannon. At one time, they had lived in the same neighborhood and had played together a lot.

At lunch, Maggie heard some of her friends gossiping about Shannon. One girl said that Shannon's clothes were ugly. Another girl added, "Yeah, and she thinks she's so smart by making a hundred in math the first day here at our school."

Maggie couldn't believe her ears because Shannon was really a sweet person!

One girl looked at Maggie and said, "I can't believe you were once friends with her. Aren't you glad that we're your friends now?"

What do you think Maggie should do?

Maggie Decides to Be *Loyal*

Maggie decided to be *loyal* to her friend Shannon. She knew that it was the right thing to do. She hoped there was a way to handle the situation so that she could keep everybody as friends.

She told her friends: "I am very glad that you all are my friends. I like you so much. About Shannon's clothes—I think we can all dress whatever way we like. Everyone has a different style, and it's really what's inside a person that counts. And Shannon is very sweet and kind. She wasn't showing off by making a hundred in math—she's just good in math. Her dad teaches math in high school. She used to help me when I got confused with a math problem. I hope that you give her a chance and get to know her."

One girl at the table, Katy, asked, "Do you think she'd explain today's math homework to me? I don't get it."

Maggie said, "I'm sure she would. Just ask her." Then Maggie changed the subject to something other than gossip. She was proud of herself for being *loyal* to her old friend.

Sandra's Story

Sandra's favorite cousin was getting married, and the cousin asked Sandra to be the flower girl at the wedding. Sandra, a fifth grader, was so excited! She would get to wear her hair pulled up with flowers in it. And, best of all, she would get to wear a beautiful pink satin dress! A friend of hers had been a flower girl and was letting her borrow the dress.

The wedding day arrived and Sandra looked lovely. The bride and groom were happy. At the wedding reception, there was a fancy cake and a bowl of strawberry punch. Everyone was enjoying them. Sandra took a cup of punch, but was too busy watching the bride and groom dance to pay attention to what she was doing. Before long, she spilled the punch on the beautiful satin dress. Sandra looked down at the red stain on the dress and began to cry. She had ruined the dress that she had borrowed.

What do you think Sandra should do?

Sandra Decides to Be *Accountable*

Sandra ran to her mother to tell her what happened. On the way, she thought of excuses she could make for why this had happened. She could lie and tell the friend who owned the dress that a stranger had accidentally knocked over the punch on her. She could try to be sneaky and return the dress folded so the stain wouldn't show.

All of a sudden, Sandra stopped that kind of thinking and decided to be *accountable* for her actions. She told her mother the truth—that she wasn't paying attention because she was watching the wedding couple dance.

Sandra's mother hugged her and said, "Let's get some club soda. Sometimes that will remove stains from fabric if you get to the stain before it dries. Sandra, we'll pay to have the dress dry-cleaned. We'll do our best to get it in perfect condition before we give it back to your friend."

They ran to the kitchen and found some club soda. To their surprise, most of the stain came out. They sent the dress to the dry cleaners as soon as possible, and Sandra used her allowance to pay the eight dollars to have the dress cleaned. She was so happy when she returned the dress. And she was very proud of herself for being *accountable* for her actions.

Mikey's Story

There were severe storms last weekend in the town where Mikey lives. In fact, a tornado touched down in a nearby town and many people's homes were destroyed. Mikey felt sorry for these people because he knew they would have to start all over again. They would need to buy clothes, furniture, kitchen supplies—just about everything! He wished he could help them, but then he thought, "I'm only a kid. What can I do?"

What do you think Mikey could do?

Mikey Decides to *Share*

Mikey told his parents how he wanted to help the people who had lost their homes to the tornado. He said, "I've got more toys than I need. I know some of the children lost all their toys and don't have anything to play with now. Would you drive me over there to give away some of my things?"

His parents told Mikey that he was kind to think about *sharing* with those in need. They added, "You know we could get some things from some of our neighbors, too. What do you think about that, Mikey?"

Mikey's mom called the City Hall in the neighboring town to ask what the people needed the most. Then Mikey put together a flyer on his computer that explained what their plans were. Mikey and his dad passed the flyers out to their neighbors and friends. Their doorbell began to ring as family after family dropped off canned goods, toys, clothing, and more! They had to use three pickup trucks to get everything to the people in need.

Mikey now knows the real value of *sharing* and really understands how happy it can make you!

CHAPTER 11

A GOOD LIFE

Mom and I talk about values

My friends, it's been so much fun learning with you about the importance of good values. We've studied being nice, involved, confident, honest, obedient, loyal, accountable, and sharing. None of these values are really hard to learn and put into practice. All we have to do is stop, think of what is the right thing to do, and then do it!

Sometimes it takes courage to do what is right, especially when other people want to do what is wrong. They may think the wrong thing will be easier. Or they may simply be lazy. Or they may have no one to teach them how to treat others. But YOU know how to be a good person.

Write to me and tell me how you're using the important values we learned in this book. My address is:

Nicholas Scott
P.O. Box 6
Weston, TX 75097

If you learn these good values and use them now while you're young, then you'll still have them when you grow up. You'll be able to make a difference in your family, your school, your town, and even your country. People will respect you and value your opinions because they know you are such a good person. I hope to keep hearing great things about you!

Love,

Nicholas

Ending Note to
Parents and Teachers

Use *Nicholas' Values: A Child's Guide to Building Character* with your child or student to initiate discussion about, and practice in, how to acquire and demonstrate important values. Here are some suggested follow-up ideas:

1. When watching television with your child, raise questions about the values that the characters are exhibiting. You can use this approach to reinforce good values (e.g., loyalty, accountability) as well as to launch discussion on what a character should be doing when the role represents unhealthy actions (e.g., dishonesty, disobedience).

2. If you notice your child struggling with one of the values in this book—for example, having trouble being loyal to a friend—resist telling the child what to do. Instead, suggest that the child re-read the chapter that focuses on that value. After this, ask the child to think about his or her decision and to discuss the issue with you. Teachers should also find this suggestion helpful with their students. Teachers should use all language processes—reading, writing, listening, and speaking— to help the students learn this material.

3. Draw on role models for further examples of the values discussed in this book. Consider:
   - Historical figures. For instance, George Washington demonstrated *honesty* by admitting he cut down the cherry tree; Martin Luther King, Jr., was *involved* by

leading the Civil Rights Movement; Mother Teresa exemplified the ultimate in *sharing* by devoting her life to those in need.

- Military or occupational figures. For instance, soldiers during wartime must be *obedient* to complete their mission safely and successfully; a firefighter must be *confident* to do his or her job.
- More personal figures. For example, friends, family, and local leaders who demonstrate these values.

4. Give praise whenever you see the child using any of these values. Make sure the praise is 100 percent positive. Avoid statements such as "It's about time you shared your toys with your brother. See how much better you get along when you do." Instead, opt for the positive: "I noticed that you were so kind to let your brother play with your toys. That was very thoughtful of you to *share*."

5. Supply your child or student with more situations similar to those in Chapter 10, "Let's Practice." Allow the child to decide how a person with good values would handle each situation.

6. Be a role model of these values yourself! Children base their actions and attitudes on our actions and attitudes. They do as we do, not as we say. Actions always speak louder than words!

ACKNOWLEDGMENT OF PERMISSIONS

Grateful acknowledgment is made to the following:

- *The Dallas Morning News,* for permission to reprint photograph by Richard Michael Pruitt, p. 65 (originally appeared *The Dallas Morning News,* June 23, 1999).
- *The Dallas Morning News,* for permission to reprint photograph by Jim Mahoney, p. 74 (originally appeared *The Dallas Morning News,* June 7, 2001).
- Marc Bekoff, for permission to base Chapter 2 on a story in *The Smile of a Dolphin,* by Marc Bekoff, copyright 2000 by Discovery Books.
- Reuters News Services, Vancouver, British Columbia, for the story of the mother duck, p. 89, published July 13, 2001.
- John Haynsworth, for photographs of the authors, p. 3 and back cover.

Contact the Author

Consider bringing family counselor Sharon Scott to your school, religious organization, retreat, or conference. She presents dynamic skills-based keynote presentations and workshops for children, teens, parents, educators, and counselors on many topics. Her presentations are filled with humor, touching stories, and empathy, and teach valuable skills that the audience can immediately use.

Sharon Scott, LPC, LMFT
LifeSkills for Positive Living
P.O. Box 6
Weston, TX 75097-0006 U.S.A.
E-mail: *sharon@peerpressure.com*
Website: *www.SharonScott.com*
Phone: 972-382-4797